Belongs to:

_____

_____

_____

My Spiritual Journey

My Spiritual Journey

A DEVOTIONAL JOURNAL

world

PUBLISHING

SINCE 1928

My
Spiritual
Journey

The peace of God is usually lost when we lose our perspective of God's overriding, unceasing care of us. . . . What troubles me and upsets my spiritual well-being, even the slightest irritant, matters to God. He is so concerned that He invites me to give Him every care.

Cast your burdens on him in prayer. Tell God what bothers you, what robs your joy and peace, and then really believe that He has heard you and will answer. If you truly trust Him to handle the problem, then experiencing His peace is a supernatural result. The situation is in God's hands. He is in control despite appearances. He is able to bring about a solution, whenever and however He chooses. When you reach that point, the peace of God is yours. The storms may brew, but God is concerned about you and has taken your cares upon Himself. When the pressure mounts, you cast every burden on Him. All is in His care, and that settles your soul as no other thought.

—*Charles Stanley*

> *If you truly trust Him to handle the problem, then experiencing His peace is a supernatural result.*

_____

_____

_____

_____

_____

_____

_____

_____

_____

_____

The man who says it cannot be done, should not interrupt the one who is doing it.

—Chinese proverb

_____

_____

_____

_____

_____

_____

_____

_____

_____

_____

_____

_____

_____

_____

_____

_____

_____

_____

_____

_____

_____

_____

BUT IF FROM THERE YOU SEEK THE LORD YOUR GOD, YOU WILL FIND HIM IF YOU LOOK FOR HIM WITH ALL YOUR HEART AND ALL YOUR SOUL.

—*Deuteronomy 4:29 NIV*

HE THAT IS

OF A MERRY HEART

HATH A CONTINUAL

FEAST.

—*Proverbs 15:15* KJV

Hope is never ill when faith is well.

—John Bunyan

Giving is an act of grace. It doesn't depend on prosperity and shouldn't be limited by our ability. It is a privilege—something we get to do—and a reflection of our own personal commitment to Christ and to His Kingdom.

—Robert J. Morgan

_____

_____

_____

_____

_____

_____

_____

_____

_____

_____

_____

_____

_____

_____

_____

_____

_____

_____

_____

_____

As every man hath received the gift, even so minister the same one to another, as good stewards of the manifold grace of God.

—1 Peter 4:10 *KJV*

_____

_____

_____

_____

_____

_____

_____

_____

_____

_____

_____

_____

_____

_____

_____

_____

_____

_____

_____

_____

CAST YOUR CARES ON THE LORD AND HE WILL SUSTAIN YOU.

—*Psalm 55:22* NIV

Faith is the first factor in a life devoted to service. Without it, nothing is possible. With it, nothing is impossible.

—Mary McLeod Bethune

_____

_____

_____

_____

_____

_____

_____

_____

_____

_____

_____

_____

_____

_____

_____

_____

_____

_____

_____

_____

_____

_____

_____

_____

Start by doing what's necessary: then do what's possible: and suddenly you are doing the impossible.

—St. Francis of Assisi

So
DON'T WORRY
ABOUT TOMOR-
ROW, FOR TOMORROW
WILL BRING ITS OWN
WORRIES. TODAY'S
TROUBLE IS ENOUGH
FOR TODAY.
—*Matthew 6:34*
CEV

I have never been much of a water drinker. . . . Then I joined a weight-loss club . . . and was told the success of the plan rested on one's commitment to drink eight glasses of water each and every day. . . . It became part of my life, a new habit that was a discipline but one from which I knew I would reap great benefits.

I considered that concept in my relationship with Christ, the Living Water. It's easy for me to spend time with the Lord in the morning and then get so caught up in the busyness of the day that it's bedtime again and I realize it's been hours since I've taken in the life-giving water of hope He offers all day long.

I have found all sorts of new ways to do that. I listen to worship tapes in my car and lift my voice in praise to God . . . I choose a verse at the beginning of the day to chew on all day long . . . I have made a practice of noticing the world around me and thanking God . . . All day long God loves to hear our needy hearts and fill our thirsty lives. Today, let's drink deeply of the one who is our hope all day long.

—*Sheila Walsh*

I have made a practice of noticing the world around me and thanking God. . .

I believe it [keeping a journal] is a very useful method to take some account of every day.

—John Newton

_____

_____

_____

_____

_____

_____

_____

_____

_____

_____

_____

_____

_____

_____

_____

_____

_____

_____

_____

_____

_____

_____

MY VOICE SHALT THOU HEAR IN THE MORNING, O LORD; IN THE MORNING WILL I DIRECT MY PRAYER UNTO THEE, AND WILL LOOK UP.

—*Psalm 5:3 KJV*

BE
STRONG AND
OF GOOD
COURAGE, DO NOT
FEAR NOR BE AFRAID OF
THEM; FOR THE LORD
YOUR GOD, HE IS THE
ONE WHO GOES WITH
YOU. HE WILL NOT LEAVE
YOU NOR FORSAKE
YOU.
—*Deuteronomy
31:6*

Write your plans in pencil but give God the eraser.
—Unknown

BEHOLD, GOD IS MY SALVATION, I WILL TRUST AND NOT BE AFRAID; FOR THE LORD GOD IS MY STRENGTH AND SONG, AND HE HAS BECOME MY SALVATION.

—*Isaiah 12:2* NASV

The best and most beautiful things in the world cannot be seen, nor touched . . . but are felt in the heart.

—Helen Keller

_____

_____

_____

_____

_____

_____

_____

_____

_____

_____

_____

_____

_____

_____

_____

_____

_____

_____

_____

_____

_____

Faith furnishes prayer with wings, without which it cannot soar to Heaven.

—St. John Climacus

LET YOUR HAND BE WITH ME, AND KEEP ME FROM HARM SO THAT I WILL BE FREE FROM PAIN.

—*1 Chronicles 4:10* NIV

How wonderful it is that nobody needs wait a single moment before starting to improve the world.
—Anne Frank

Every happening, great and small, is a parable whereby God speaks to us, and the art of life is to get the message.
—Malcolm Muggeridge

LOVE YOUR ENEMIES, BLESS THEM THAT CURSE YOU, DO GOOD TO THEM THAT HATE YOU, AND PRAY FOR THEM WHICH DESPITEFULLY USE YOU, AND PERSECUTE YOU; THAT YE MAY BE THE CHILDREN OF YOUR FATHER WHICH IS IN HEAVEN.

—*Matthew 5:44–48 KJV*

To give without any reward, or any notice, has a special quality of its own.

—Anne Morrow Lindbergh

Being gentle doesn't mean

being weak or fragile. It just means that we are moderate in our reactions, we temper our responses, we try to see things from the other person's point of view, and we act and speak out of maturity and love. When we do that, it tends to reduce stress in our interpersonal relationships, and that lowers the levels of anxiety and worry we bear.

So if you are struggling with worry today, take the Bible's advice: Rejoice in the Lord always. Let your gentleness be evident to all. Remember that the Lord is near. Don't worry about anything, but in everything by prayer and petition with thanksgiving, let your requests be made known to God. And set your mind on those things that are excellent and praiseworthy. And the God of peace will be with you.

—Robert J. Morgan

Rejoice in the Lord always. Let your gentleness be evident to all. Remember that the Lord is near.

The purpose of life is to live a life of purpose.
—Robert Byrne

_____

_____

_____

_____

_____

_____

_____

_____

_____

_____

_____

_____

_____

_____

_____

_____

_____

_____

_____

HE WHO GIVES HEED TO THE WORD WILL PROSPER, AND HAPPY IS HE WHO TRUSTS IN THE LORD.

—*Proverbs 16:20* NRSV

If God has given you life abundantly, why aren't you using it?

—Luci Swindoll

IN THE DAY WHEN I CRIED OUT, YOU ANSWERED ME, AND MADE ME BOLD WITH STRENGTH IN MY SOUL.

—*Psalm 138:3*

I SEARCHED EVERYWHERE, DETERMINED TO FIND WISDOM AND TO UNDERSTAND THE REASON FOR THINGS. I WAS DETERMINED TO PROVE TO MYSELF THAT WICKEDNESS IS STUPID AND THAT FOOLISHNESS IS MADNESS.

—*Ecclesiastes 7:25* NLT

Beware of no man more than of yourself: we carry our worst enemies within us.

—Charles Haddon Spurgeon

At the beginning of every act of faith, there is often a seed of fear.
For great acts of faith are seldom born out of calm calculation.
—Max Lucado

I SOUGHT THE LORD, AND HE HEARD ME, AND DELIVERED ME FROM ALL MY FEARS.

—Psalm 34:4

_____

_____

_____

_____

_____

_____

_____

_____

_____

_____

_____

_____

_____

_____

_____

_____

_____

_____

_____

_____

_____

_____

The shortest distance between a problem and a solution is the distance
between your knees and the floor.
—Charles Stanley

You change your life by changing your heart.
—Max Lucado

I LOVE THE LORD, BECAUSE HE HAS HEARD MY VOICE AND MY SUPPLICATIONS. BECAUSE HE HAS INCLINED HIS EAR TO ME, THEREFORE I WILL CALL UPON HIM AS LONG AS I LIVE.

—*Psalm 116:1–2*

'Let
your conscience
be your guide' is
valid only if God's
Word is guiding your
conscience.
—Unknown

Do not be anxious about anything, but in everything, by prayer and petition, with thanksgiving, present your requests to God.

And the peace of God, which transcends all understanding, will guard your hearts and your minds in Christ Jesus.

Finally, brothers, whatever is true, whatever is noble, whatever is right, whatever is pure, whatever is lovely, whatever is admirable—if anything is excellent or praiseworthy—think about such things.

—*Philippians 4:6–8*

Whatever is right, whatever is pure, whatever is lovely, whatever is admirable—if anything is excellent or praiseworthy—think about such things.

The chains of habit are generally too small to be felt until they are too strong to be broken.

—Samuel Johnson

_____

_____

_____

_____

_____

_____

_____

_____

_____

_____

_____

_____

_____

_____

_____

_____

_____

_____

_____

AND DO NOT BE CONFORMED TO THIS WORLD, BUT BE TRANSFORMED BY THE RENEWING OF YOUR MIND, THAT YOU MAY PROVE WHAT IS THAT GOOD AND ACCEPTABLE AND PERFECT WILL OF GOD.

—*Romans 12:2*

My Presence will go with you, and I will give you rest.

—*Exodus 33:14*

If two people agree on everything, one of them is unnecessary.
—Ruth Bell Graham

LOVE THE LORD YOUR GOD WITH ALL YOUR HEART AND WITH ALL YOUR SOUL AND WITH ALL YOUR STRENGTH.

—*Deuteronomy 6:5*

Little faith will bring your soul to heaven; great faith will bring heaven to your soul.
—Unknown

Changing directions in life is not tragic; losing passion in life is.
—Max Lucado

Jesus is God spelling himself out in language
that man can understand.

—S. D. Gordon

Constant kindness can accomplish much. As the sun makes ice melt, kindness causes misunderstanding, mistrust, and hostility to evaporate.
—Albert Schweitzer

O

COME, LET US

WORSHIP AND BOW

DOWN; LET US KNEEL

BEFORE THE LORD

OUR MAKER.

—*Psalm 95:6*

God gave us the gift of free will. We have the power to choose. We may not have a choice about what happens in certain situations, but we can choose how we respond. No matter what we face in life, God enables us to learn and grow from our choices. "Good and evil both increase at compound interest. That is why the little decisions you and I make every day are of such infinite importance," C. S. Lewis said. "Every time you make a choice you are turning the central part of you, the part that chooses, into something a little different than it was before."

Meditating on God's Word can help you make wise choices that lead to holy living. God promises that He will give you the strength and wisdom you need. . . . You can make courageous choices that will result in positive change, healthy self-esteem, spiritual stamina, and a more fulfilling life.

—*Checklist for Life for Women*

Meditating on God's Word can help you make wise choices that lead to holy living.

Trust God's authority, not man's majority.
—Unknown

_____

GOD IS LOVE, AND HE WHO ABIDES IN LOVE ABIDES IN GOD, AND GOD IN HIM.

—*1 John 4:16 NASV*

IN MY FATHER'S HOUSE ARE MANY MANSIONS. IF IT WERE NOT SO, I WOULD HAVE TOLD YOU. I GO TO PREPARE A PLACE FOR YOU.

—*John 14:1–2*

ENTER INTO HIS GATES WITH THANKSGIVING, AND INTO HIS COURTS WITH PRAISE: BE THANKFUL UNTO HIM, AND BLESS HIS NAME.

—*Psalm 100:4* KJV

I have a great hunger to know God, to learn how to love, to care for the part of my life that is eternal.
—Sheila Walsh

_____

_____

_____

_____

_____

_____

_____

_____

_____

_____

_____

_____

_____

_____

_____

_____

_____

_____

_____

_____

_____

_____

_____

As you walk through the valley of the unknown, you will find the footprints of Jesus both in front of you and beside you.
—Charles Stanley

DO NOT STORE UP FOR YOURSELVES TREASURES ON EARTH, WHERE MOTH AND RUST DESTROY, AND WHERE THIEVES BREAK IN AND STEAL. BUT STORE UP FOR YOURSELVES TREASURES IN HEAVEN, WHERE MOTH AND RUST DO NOT DESTROY, AND WHERE THIEVES DO NOT BREAK IN AND STEAL. FOR WHERE YOUR TREASURE IS, THERE YOUR HEART WILL BE ALSO.

—Matthew 6:19–21

No smile is as beautiful as the one that struggles through tears.
—Unknown

The beginning of anxiety is the end of faith; and the beginning of true faith is the end of anxiety.
—George Mueller

If God is not first in our thoughts and efforts in the mornings, He will be in last place the rest of the day.

—E. M. Bounds

_____

_____

_____

_____

_____

_____

_____

_____

_____

_____

_____

_____

_____

_____

_____

_____

_____

_____

_____

_____

_____

BUT WHEN
YOU DO GOOD AND
SUFFER, IF YOU TAKE IT
PATIENTLY, THIS IS
COMMENDABLE
BEFORE GOD.
—*2 Peter 2:20*

If I speak in the tongues of men and of angels, but have not love, I am only a resounding gong or a clanging cymbal. If I have the gift of prophecy and can fathom all mysteries and all knowledge, and if I have a faith that can move mountains, but have not love, I am nothing. If I give all I possess to the poor and surrender my body to the flames, but have not love I gain nothing. Love is patient, love is kind. It does not envy, it does not boast, it is not proud. It is not rude, it is not self-seeking, it is not easily angered, it keeps no record of wrongs. Love does not delight in evil but rejoices with the truth. It always protects, always trusts, always perseveres. Love never fails. But where there are prophecies, they will cease; where there are tongues, they will be stilled; where there is knowledge, it will pass away . . . And now these things remain: faith, hope and love. But the greatest of these is love.

—*1 Corinthians 13:1-8, 13 NIV*

LOVE IS PATIENT, LOVE IS KIND. IT DOES NOT ENVY, IT DOES NOT BOAST, IT IS NOT PROUD. IT IS NOT RUDE, IT IS NOT SELF-SEEKING, IT IS NOT EASILY ANGERED, IT KEEPS NO RECORD OF WRONGS.

The Word of God is a powerful sword of an upright man.
—José B. Cabajar

_____

_____

_____

_____

_____

_____

_____

_____

_____

_____

_____

_____

_____

_____

_____

_____

_____

_____

_____

_____

_____

_____

_____

_____

FOR GOD SO LOVED THE WORLD, THAT HE GAVE HIS ONLY BEGOTTEN SON, THAT WHOSOEVER BELIEVETH IN HIM SHOULD NOT PERISH, BUT HAVE EVERLASTING LIFE.

—*John 3:16 KJV*

REFRAIN FROM
ANGER AND TURN
FROM WRATH; DO NOT
FRET—IT LEADS ONLY
TO EVIL.
—*Psalm 37:8* NIV

When you can't trace His hand you can trust His heart.
—Charles Haddon Spurgeon

_____

_____

_____

_____

_____

_____

_____

_____

_____

_____

_____

_____

_____

_____

_____

_____

_____

_____

_____

_____

_____

_____

_____

_____

You can give without loving, but you cannot love without giving.
—Amy Carmichael

GOD BLESSES THOSE WHOSE HEARTS ARE PURE, FOR THEY WILL SEE GOD.

—*Matthew 5:8* NLT

Finish every day and be done with it. You have done what you could. Some blunders and absurdities no doubt have crept in; forget them as soon as you can. Tomorrow is a new day; begin it well and serenely and with too high a spirit to be cumbered with your old nonsense. This day is all that is good and fair. It is too dear, with its hopes and invitations, to waste a moment on yesterdays.

—Ralph Waldo Emerson

THE LORD WILL GUIDE YOU ALWAYS; HE WILL SATISFY YOUR NEEDS IN A SUN-SCORCHED LAND AND WILL STRENGTHEN YOUR FRAME.

—*Isaiah 58:11 NIV*

Sometimes God has to put us flat on our back before we are looking up to Him.

—Dr. Jack Graham

The Bible is . . . as necessary to spiritual life as breath is to natural life. There is nothing more essential to our lives than the Word of God.

—Jack Hayford

_____

_____

_____

_____

_____

_____

_____

_____

_____

_____

_____

_____

_____

_____

_____

_____

_____

_____

_____

_____

Because God is everywhere, you can pray anywhere.
—Unknown

Keep Holding onto What is Right

From my Promise Book on February 3, 1968:

Continue to keep a firm hold on my professions of faith in Christ.
Continue coming with courage to the throne of God to obtain
mercy and spiritual strength when I need it.
Continue progressing toward maturity.
Continue filling my mind with the things above, not with
things on earth.
Continue to find and follow God's will—what is well
pleasing to Him.
Continue to show the same earnestness to the very
end so I may enjoy my hope to the fullest.

—*Luci Swindoll*

> *Continue filling my mind with the things above, not with things on earth.*

_____

_____

_____

_____

_____

_____

_____

_____

_____

_____

_____

_____

_____

If we were given all we wanted here, our hearts would settle for this world rather than the next.

—Elisabeth Elliot

_____
_____
_____
_____
_____
_____
_____
_____
_____
_____
_____
_____
_____
_____
_____
_____
_____
_____
_____

IN ALL THIS I HAVE GIVEN YOU AN EXAMPLE THAT BY SUCH WORK WE MUST SUPPORT THE WEAK, REMEMBERING THE WORDS OF THE LORD JESUS, FOR HE HIMSELF SAID, "IT IS MORE BLESSED TO GIVE THAN TO RECEIVE."

—Acts 20:35 NRSV

AND
WE KNOW
THAT ALL THINGS
WORK TOGETHER FOR
GOOD TO THOSE WHO
LOVE GOD, TO THOSE
WHO ARE THE CALLED
ACCORDING TO HIS
PURPOSE.
—*Romans 8:28*

I know the Bible is inspired because it inspires me.

—Dwight L. Moody

Never think that God's delays are God's denials. Hold on: hold fast: hold out. Patience is genius.
—George-Louis Leclerc de Buffon

_____

_____

_____

_____

_____

_____

_____

_____

_____

_____

_____

_____

_____

_____

_____

_____

_____

_____

_____

_____

_____

_____

THE LORD SHATTERS THE PLANS OF THE NATIONS AND THWARTS ALL THEIR SCHEMES. BUT THE LORD'S PLANS STAND FIRM FOREVER; HIS INTENTIONS CAN NEVER BE SHAKEN.

—*Psalm 33:10–11 NLT*

The stars may fall, but God's promises will stand and be fulfilled.
—J. I. Packer

HAVE I NOT COMMANDED YOU? BE STRONG AND COURAGEOUS. DO NOT BE TERRIFIED; DO NOT BE DISCOURAGED, FOR THE LORD YOUR GOD WILL BE WITH YOU WHEREVER YOU GO.

—*Joshua 1:9* NIV

Heaven is under our feet as well as over our heads.
—Henry David Thoreau

Kind words do not cost much. They never blister the tongue or lips. They make other people good-natured. They also produce their own image on men's souls, and a beautiful image it is.

—Blaise Pascal

THIS IS THE DAY WHICH THE LORD HATH MADE; WE WILL REJOICE AND BE GLAD IN IT.

—*Psalm 118:24* KJV

It is no use walking any-where to preach unless our walking is our preaching.

—St. Francis of Assisi

Peacemaking is a noble

vocation. But you can no more make peace in your own strength than a mason can build a wall without a trowel, a carpenter build a house without a hammer, or an artist paint a picture without a brush. You must have the proper equipment. To be a peacemaker, you must know the Peace Giver. To make peace on earth, you must know the peace of heaven. You must know Him who is our peace.

—Billy Graham

To make peace on earth, you must know the peace of heaven.

Submission to God's will is the softest pillow on which to rest.

—Unknown

_____

_____

_____

_____

_____

_____

_____

_____

_____

_____

_____

_____

_____

_____

_____

_____

_____

_____

_____

_____

_____

_____

I TRUST IN THE MERCY OF GOD FOREVER AND EVER.

—Psalm 52:8

If the bottom falls out of our world, there is only one place for us to land and that is in God's lap.
—Unknown

COME UNTO ME, ALL YE THAT LABOR AND ARE HEAVY LADEN, AND I WILL GIVE YOU REST.

—*Matthew 11:28* KJV

God has two dwellings; one in heaven, and the other in a meek and thankful heart.
—Izaak Walton

THE LORD YOUR GOD WILL BLESS YOU IN ALL YOUR PRODUCE AND IN ALL THE WORK OF YOUR HANDS, SO THAT YOU SURELY REJOICE.

—Deuteronomy 16:15

HE THAT DWELLETH IN THE SECRET PLACE OF THE MOST HIGH SHALL ABIDE IN THE SHADOW OF THE ALMIGHTY. I WILL SAY OF THE LORD, HE IS MY REFUGE AND MY FORTRESS: MY GOD; IN HIM WILL I TRUST.

—*Psalm 91:1-2 KJV*

The times we find ourselves having to wait on others may be the perfect opportunities to train ourselves to wait on the Lord.

—Joni Eareckson Tada

_____

_____

_____

_____

_____

_____

_____

_____

_____

_____

_____

_____

_____

_____

_____

_____

_____

_____

_____

_____

_____

_____

_____

_____

_____

AS FOR ME AND MY HOUSE, WE WILL SERVE THE LORD.

—*Joshua 24:15*

It is not doing the thing which we like to do, but liking the thing we have to do, that makes life blessed.

—Goethe

Everything Has Its Time

To everything there is a season,
A time for every purpose under heaven:
A time to be born, and a time to die;
A time to plant, and a time to pluck up what is planted;
A time to kill, and a time to heal;
A time to break down, and a time to build up;
A time to weep, and a time to laugh;
A time to mourn, and a time to dance;
A time to throw away stones, And a time to gather stones together;
A time to embrace, And a time to refrain from embracing;
A time to seek, and a time to lose;
A time to keep, and a time to throw away;
A time to tear, and a time to sew;
A time to keep silence, and a time to speak;
A time to love, and a time to hate,
A time for war, and a time for peace.

—*Ecclesiastes 3: 1-8*

A time to mourn, and a time to dance; A time to embrace, And a time to refrain from embracing; A time to seek, and a time to lose; A time to keep, and a time to throw away. . .

To love another person is to see the face of God.

—Victor Hugo

God would be pleased if you were to take one last look in the mirror before you start your day and say, "God loves you . . . and so do I."

—Zig Ziglar

FINALLY, BRETHREN, WHATEVER THINGS ARE TRUE, WHATEVER THINGS ARE NOBLE, WHATEVER THINGS ARE JUST, WHATEVER THINGS ARE PURE, WHATEVER THINGS ARE LOVELY, WHATEVER THINGS ARE OF GOOD REPORT, IF THERE IS ANY VIRTUE AND IF THERE IS ANYTHING PRAISE-WORTHY, MEDITATE ON THESE THINGS.

—Philippians 4:8

Don't say you don't have enough time. You have exactly the same number of hours per day that were given to Helen Keller, Pasteur, Michaelangelo, Mother Teresa, Leonardo da Vinci, Thomas Jefferson, and Albert Einstein.

—H. Jackson Brown

MAKE A JOYFUL NOISE UNTO THE LORD, ALL YE LANDS. SERVE THE LORD WITH GLADNESS: COME BEFORE HIS PRESENCE WITH SINGING.

—Psalm 100:1-2 KJV

No one can make you feel inferior without your consent.
—Eleanor Roosevelt

AND WHEN YOU STAND PRAYING, IF YOU HOLD ANYTHING AGAINST ANYONE, FORGIVE HIM,
SO THAT YOUR FATHER IN HEAVEN MAY FORGIVE YOU YOUR SINS.

—*Mark 11:25* NIV

THE LORD IS NEAR TO ALL WHO CALL ON HIM, TO ALL WHO CALL ON HIM IN TRUTH.

—*Psalm 145:18* NIV

If you carry a Bible when you are young, it will carry you when are old.
—Unknown

BEHOLD, I STAND AT THE DOOR, AND KNOCK: IF ANY MAN HEAR MY VOICE, AND OPEN THE DOOR, I WILL COME IN TO HIM, AND WILL SUP WITH HIM, AND HE WITH ME.

—*Revelation 3:20 KJV*

A keen
sense of humor
helps us to overlook
the unbecoming,
understand the
unconventional,
tolerate the unpleasant,
overcome the
unexpected, and out-
last the unbearable.

—Billy Graham

There is a big difference between thinking and obsessing. . . .When we are obsessing, we are in great danger of being consumed by our thoughts and feelings. We might let our fear overtake us or let our past get the best of us. . . . Obsessing is not productive; it's destructive. It carves grooves in our minds that allow the tired scripts to keep running.

Thinking sets us free as we ponder God's love for us. It opens the whole universe to us instead of one little groove. It enables us to move forward in our lives toward the relationship with God that our hearts were made for.

God loves you and that changes everything. . . . His compassion doesn't run out. You can have real hope because God is faithful—even when you haven't been. He did not ask you to carry the burden of the faithfulness part; He promised to do that for you.

—Nicole Johnson

God loves you and that changes everything. . . . His compassion doesn't run out. You can have real hope because God is faithful—even when you haven't been.

Anxiety does not empty tomorrow of its sorrows, but only empties today of its strength.

—Charles Haddon Spurgeon

Faith
is deliberate
confidence in the
character of God
whose ways you may
not understand at
the time.
—Oswald
Chambers

FOR THE LORD SEARCHES ALL HEARTS AND UNDERSTANDS ALL THE INTENT OF THE THOUGHTS. IF YOU SEEK HIM, HE WILL BE FOUND BY YOU; BUT IF YOU FORSAKE HIM, HE WILL CAST YOU OFF FOREVER.

—1 Chronicles 28:9

God has promised strength for the day, rest for the labor, light for the way, grace for the trials, help from above, unfailing sympathy, undying love.

—Annie Johnson Flint

LOVE DOES NOT DELIGHT IN EVIL BUT REJOICES WITH THE TRUTH.

—*1 Corinthians 13:6* NIV

God's Word is as good as He is. There is an old saying that a man is as good as his word. Well, God is as good as His Word. His character is behind what He has said.

—J. Vernon McGee

If you refuse to give up, you cannot fail.
—Nicole Johnson, Miss America 1999

When you are in the furnace, your Father keeps His eye on the clock and His hand on the thermostat. He knows just how much we can take.

—Warren W. Wiersbe

_____

_____

_____

_____

_____

_____

_____

_____

_____

_____

_____

_____

_____

_____

_____

_____

_____

_____

_____

_____

_____

_____

*K*ind hearts are the gardens,
Kind thoughts are the roots,
Kind words are the flowers,
Kind deeds are the fruits,

Take care of your garden
And keep out the weeds,
Fill it with sunshine
Kind words and kind deeds.

—Henry Wadsworth Longfellow

DON'T FORGET TO SHOW HOSPITALITY TO STRANGERS, FOR SOME WHO HAVE DONE THIS HAVE ENTERTAINED ANGELS WITHOUT REALIZING IT.

—Hebrews 13:2

NLT

Conscience is condensed character.
—Unknown

All my life I have been looking for a pot of gold at the end of a rainbow, and I found it at the foot of the cross.
—Dale Evans Rogers

THE LORD IS MY SHEPHERD; I SHALL NOT WANT. HE MAKETH ME TO LIE DOWN IN GREEN PASTURES: HE LEADETH ME BESIDE THE STILL WATERS. HE RESTORETH MY SOUL.

—*Psalm 23:1-3 KJV*

Be kind and merciful. Let no one ever come to you without coming away better and happier. Be the living expression of God's kindness.
—Mother Teresa

EVERYTHING COMES FROM YOU, AND WE HAVE GIVEN YOU ONLY WHAT COMES FROM YOUR HAND.

—*1 Chronicles 29:14b* NIV

Nature is an unlimited broadcasting station, through which God speaks to us every hour, if we only will tune in.
—George Washington Carver

FORGIVE, AND ACT, AND GIVE TO EVERYONE ACCORDING TO ALL HIS WAYS, WHOSE HEART
YOU KNOW (FOR YOU ALONE KNOW THE HEARTS OF ALL THE SONS OF MEN).

—*1 Kings 8:39*

Every evening I turn my worries over to God. He's going to be up all night anyway.
—Mary C. Crowley

As much of heaven is visible as we have eyes to see.
—William Winter

SO THEN FAITH COMES BY HEARING, AND HEARING BY THE WORD OF GOD.

—Romans 10:17

David wasn't thinking of being king when he was tending sheep; he was just doing what God sat before him.
—John Fischer

*L*et nothing disturb me,
Let nothing frighten me,
Let nothing take away my peace.
May I wait with trust, with patience,
knowing you will provide for me.
I lack for nothing in You, God.
You are my strong foundation,
You are enough for me.

—*Teresa of Avila*

IN GOD, WHOSE WORD I PRAISE, IN GOD I TRUST; I WILL NOT BE AFRAID. WHAT CAN MORTAL MAN DO TO ME?

—*Psalm 56:4*

Faith is like radar that sees through the fog.
—Corrie ten Boom

Difficulties are meant to rouse, not discourage. The human spirit is to grow strong by conflict.
—William Ellery Channing

HOW GOOD AND PLEASANT IT IS WHEN BROTHERS LIVE TOGETHER IN UNITY!

—Psalm 133:1 NIV

Gratitude unlocks the fullness of life. It turns what we have into enough, and more.
—Melody Beattie

LET YOUR CONDUCT BE WITHOUT COVETOUSNESS; BE CONTENT WITH SUCH THINGS AS YOU
HAVE. FOR HE HIMSELF HAS SAID, "I WILL NEVER LEAVE YOU NOR FORSAKE YOU."

—Hebrews 13:5

God always answers our prayer. Either He changes the circum-
stances, or He supplies sufficient power to overcome them.
—Unknown

DO NOT LOVE THE WORLD OR THE THINGS THAT ARE IN THE WORLD. IF ANYONE LOVES THE WORLD, THE LOVE OF THE FATHER IS NOT IN HIM.

—*1 John 2:15*

God loves each of us as if there were only one of us.
—Augustine

We make a living by what we get. We make a life by what we give.
—Sir Winston Churchill

GIVE US HELP FROM TROUBLE.

—*Psalm 60:11* KJV

God never changes moods or cools off in His affections or loses enthusiasm.

—A. W. Tozer

For I am persuaded

that neither death nor life,
nor angels nor principalities nor powers,
nor things present nor things to come,
nor height nor depth,
nor any other created thing,
shall be able to separate us from the love of God
which is in Christ Jesus our Lord.

—*Romans 8:38–39*

*God
doesn't look at how
much we do, but with
how much love
we do it.*

—Mother Teresa

How many are your works, O Lord! In wisdom you made them all; the earth is full of your creatures. There is the sea, vast and spacious, teeming with creatures beyond number — living things both large and small.

—Psalm 104:24–25 NIV

Every calling is great when greatly pursued.
—Oliver Wendell Holmes

LET YOUR LIGHT SHINE BEFORE MEN, THAT THEY MAY SEE YOUR GOOD WORKS, AND GLORIFY YOUR FATHER WHICH IS IN HEAVEN.

—*Matthew 5:16 KJV*

Reason is our soul's left hand, Faith her right.
—John Donne

ANXIETY IN THE HEART OF MAN CAUSES DEPRESSION, BUT A GOOD WORD MAKES IT GLAD.

—*Proverbs 12:25*

True thanksgiving means that we need to thank God for what He has done for us, and not to tell Him what we have done for Him.

—George R. Hendrick

GOD WILL WIPE AWAY EVERY TEAR FROM THEIR EYES; THERE SHALL BE NO MORE DEATH, NOR SORROW, NOR CRYING. THERE SHALL BE NO MORE PAIN, FOR THE FORMER THINGS HAVE PASSED AWAY.

—*Revelation 21:4*

God understands our prayers even when we can't find the words to say them.

—Unknown

Happiness cannot be traveled to, owned, earned, worn or consumed. Happiness is the spiritual experience of living every minute with love, grace and gratitude.

—Denis Waitley

IF ANY OF YOU LACKS WISDOM, LET HIM ASK OF GOD, WHO GIVES TO ALL LIBERALLY AND WITHOUT REPROACH, AND IT WILL BE GIVEN TO HIM.

—*James 1:5*

*Commitment
in the face of
challenge produces
character.*
—John C. Maxwell

*D*o not pray for easy lives; pray to be stronger people!
Do not pray for tasks equal to your powers;
pray for powers equal to your tasks,
then what you do in your world shall be no miracle,
but you shall be a miracle.
Everyday you shall wonder at yourself,
at the richness of life,
which has come to you by the grace of God.

—*Phillips Brooks*

The world is full of suffering. It is also full of the overcoming of it.
—Helen Keller

What we are is God's gift to us. What we become is our gift to God.
—Eleanor Powell

Happiness is an emotion, and joy is an attitude. Emotions come and go, but attitudes come and grow.
—Robert J. Morgan

The greatest mistake we make is living in constant fear that we will make one.

—John Maxwell

LORD, WHO MAY DWELL IN YOUR SANCTUARY? . . . HE WHOSE WALK IS BLAMELESS AND WHO DOES WHAT IS RIGHTEOUS . . . WHO KEEPS HIS OATH, EVEN WHEN IT HURTS.

—Psalm 15:1-2, 4 NIV

We are all faced with a series of great opportunities brilliantly disguised as impossible situations.
—Charles Swindoll

He who is filled with love is filled with God himself.

—Augustine

Often, in the midst of great problems, we stop short of the real blessing God has for us, which is a fresh vision of who He is.

—Anne Graham Lotz

_____
_____
_____
_____
_____
_____
_____
_____
_____
_____

> WHEN
> I WAS A CHILD,
> I SPOKE AS A CHILD,
> I UNDERSTOOD AS A
> CHILD, I THOUGHT AS A
> CHILD; BUT WHEN I
> BECAME A MAN, I PUT
> AWAY CHILDISH
> THINGS.
> —*1 Corinthians
> 13:11*

_____
_____
_____
_____
_____
_____
_____
_____

I know that the will of God is not some mysterious thing that only a few select people can understand. It's there for each one of us, but we have to take the necessary steps to find it. The steps are simple, but often for that very reason we don't bother to take them. Yet we *have* to take them because we can never be happy until we understand God's will for our lives and are living it.

Until we are living in the will of God, we are destined to have lives that are unfulfilled and incomplete. Knowing that God has a plan for you gives your life purpose as nothing else can. It simplifies everything because you don't have to figure it all out and make it all happen. You just have to look to the Lord, knowing *He* has it all figured out and *He* will make it happen.

—*Stormie Omartian*

It's there for each one of us, but we have to take the necessary steps to find it. The steps are simple, but often for that very reason we don't bother to take them.

When we long for life without difficulties, remember that oaks grow strong in contrary winds, and diamonds are made under pressure.
—Peter Marshall

_____

_____

_____

_____

_____

_____

_____

_____

_____

_____

_____

_____

_____

_____

_____

_____

_____

_____

_____

_____

_____

_____

BLESSED ARE THOSE WHO KEEP HIS TESTIMONIES, WHO SEEK HIM WITH THE WHOLE HEART!
—*Psalm 119:2*

_If you judge
people, you have
no time
to love them._
—Mother Teresa

THOSE THAT WAIT UPON THE LORD SHALL RENEW THEIR STRENGTH.

—*Isaiah 40:31*

To us also, through every star, through every blade of grass, is not God made visible if we will open our minds and our eyes?
—Thomas Carlyle

FEASTS ARE MADE FOR LAUGHTER.

—*Ecclesiastes 10:19* NRSV

Worshipping in all the moments of our lives changes us because we move from trying to be perfect to resting in the perfect will of a God who loves us passionately.

—Sheila Walsh

If you can learn to laugh in spite of the circumstances that surround you, you will enrich others, enrich yourself, and more than that, you will last!

—Barbara Johnson

HE HEALS THE HEARTBROKEN . . . HE COUNTS THE STARS AND ASSIGNS EACH A NAME. OUR LORD IS GREAT, WITH LIMITLESS STRENGTH; WE'LL NEVER COMPREHEND WHAT HE KNOWS AND DOES.

—*Psalm 147: 3-5 NIV*

A good man is not a perfect man; a good man is an honest man, faithful, and unhesitatingly responsive to the voice of God in his life.

—John Fischer

*Lord,*
make me an instrument of your peace.
Where there is hatred,
let me sow love;
where there is injury, pardon;
where there is doubt, faith;
where there is despair, hope;
where there is darkness, light;
and where there is sadness, joy.

—*St. Francis of Assisi*

TAKE MY YOKE UPON YOU AND LEARN FROM ME, FOR I AM GENTLE AND HUMBLE IN HEART, AND YOU WILL FIND REST FOR YOUR SOULS. FOR MY YOKE IS EASY AND MY BURDEN IS LIGHT.
—*Matthew 11:29–30*

Don't duck the most difficult problems. That just insures that the hardest part will be left when you're most tired. Get the big one done — it's downhill from then on.

—Norman Vincent Peale

When all else is gone, God is left, and nothing changes Him.

—Hannah Whitall Smith

GIVE THANKS TO THE LORD, FOR HIS LOVE ENDURES FOREVER.

—*2 Chronicles 20:21* NIV

Belief is truth held in the mind; faith is a fire in the heart.
—Joseph Fort Newton

FOR WHAT PROFIT IS IT TO A MAN IF HE GAINS THE WHOLE WORLD, AND LOSES HIS OWN SOUL? OR WHAT WILL A MAN GIVE IN EXCHANGE FOR HIS SOUL?

—*Matthew 16:26*

God will not look you over for medals, degrees or diplomas, but for scars.
—Elbert Hubbard

LET THE WORD OF CHRIST DWELL IN YOU RICHLY; TEACH AND ADMONISH ONE ANOTHER IN ALL WISDOM; AND WITH GRATITUDE IN YOUR HEARTS SING PSALMS, HYMNS, AND SPIRITUAL SONGS TO GOD.

—Colossians 3:16 NRSV

PEACE I LEAVE WITH YOU; MY PEACE I GIVE YOU. I DO NOT GIVE TO YOU AS THE WORLD GIVES. DO NOT LET YOUR HEARTS BE TROUBLED AND DO NOT BE AFRAID.

—*John 14:27* NIV

By living fully, recognizing that all we do is by His power, we honor God; He in turn blesses us.

—Becky Laird

_____

_____

_____

_____

_____

_____

_____

_____

_____

_____

_____

_____

_____

_____

_____

_____

_____

_____

_____

_____

_____

_____

_____

_____

You are my hiding place; You will protect me from trouble and surround me with songs of deliverance.

—*Psalm 32:7 NIV*

*Doubts are the
ants in the pants of
faith. They keep it
awake and moving.*
—Frederick Buechner

How often, while being

pulled in all directions, do we momentarily doubt God's power and presence and concern. If God really loved me, why would he let this happen? Does He care?

So what is the antidote for being pulled in all directions, for doubting God's goodness, for brooding, for being worried and for being upset about many things? The antidote is learning to sit at Jesus' feet, soaking up the divine, infallible words given to us in His Holy Bible. We can do that by spending an occasional day in prayer, by cultivating our daily quiet time, by attending church regularly, and by letting our last conscious thought every evening be Scripture.

The antidote is learning to sit at Jesus' feet, soaking up the divine, infallible words given to us in His Holy Bible.

When we do that, it makes a difference. The pressures and problems of life are reduced to their proper dimensions in our minds, and the Lord gives us His insight, His wisdom, His strength.

—*Robert J. Morgan*

_____

_____

_____

_____

_____

_____

_____

_____

_____

_____

When we let God's Word seep into our own lives little by little … it nourishes us and becomes part of us.
—Janette Oke

Most people who succeed in the face of seemingly impossible conditions are people who simply don't know how to quit.
—Robert Schuller

BEHOLD, CHILDREN ARE A BLESSING FROM THE LORD. THE FRUIT OF THE WOMB IS A REWARD. LIKE THE ARROWS IN THE HAND OF A WARRIOR, SO ARE THE CHILDREN OF ONE'S YOUTH. HAPPY IS THE MAN WHO HAS HIS QUIVER FULL OF THEM.

—Psalm 127:3-5

If you can't be thankful for what you receive,
be thankful for what you escape.
—Unknown

_____

_____

_____

_____

_____

_____

_____

_____

_____

_____

_____

_____

_____

_____

_____

_____

_____

_____

_____

_____

_____

My kindness is all you need. My power is strongest when you are weak.
—*2 Corinthians 12:9* CEV

_____

_____

_____

_____

_____

_____

_____

_____

_____

_____

_____

_____

_____

_____

_____

_____

_____

_____

_____

_____

_____

_____

IF YOU OBEY MY COMMANDS, YOU WILL REMAIN IN MY LOVE, JUST AS I HAVE OBEYED MY FATHER'S COMMANDS AND REMAIN IN HIS LOVE. I HAVE TOLD YOU THIS SO THAT MY JOY MAY BE IN YOU AND THAT YOUR JOY MAY BE COMPLETE. MY COMMAND IS THIS: LOVE EACH OTHER AS I HAVE LOVED YOU.

—*John 15:10-12* NIV

Faith, mighty faith, the promise sees, And looks to God alone;
Laughs at impossibilities, And cries it shall be done.
—Charles Wesley

The truth is that our trials are a furnace forging us into gold.
—Barbara Johnson

I
TELL YOU
THE TRUTH, IF
YOU HAVE FAITH AS
SMALL AS A MUSTARD
SEED, YOU CAN SAY TO
THIS MOUNTAIN, 'MOVE
FROM HERE TO THERE'
AND IT WILL MOVE.
— *Matthew 17:20*
NIV

Do not fret because of evildoers,
Nor be envious of the workers of iniquity.
For they shall soon be cut down like the grass,
And wither as the green herb.
Trust in the Lord, and do good;
Dwell in the land, and feed on His faithfulness.
Delight yourself also in the Lord,
And He shall give you the desires of your heart.
Commit your way to the Lord,
Trust also in Him, and He shall bring it to pass . . .
Rest in the Lord, and wait patiently for Him;
Do not fret because of him who prospers in his way . . .
Cease from anger, and forsake wrath;
Do not fret—it only causes harm.

—Psalm 37:1–8

TRUST IN THE LORD, AND DO GOOD; DWELL IN THE LAND, AND FEED ON HIS FAITHFULNESS. DELIGHT YOURSELF ALSO IN THE LORD, AND HE SHALL GIVE YOU THE DESIRES OF YOUR HEART.

Nothing is more honorable than a grateful heart.

—Seneca

The satisfaction that accompanies good acts is itself not the motivation of the act; satisfaction is not the motive, but only the consequence.

—Bishop Joseph Butler

I DELIGHT TO DO YOUR WILL, O MY GOD, AND YOUR LAW IS WITHIN MY HEART.

—Psalm 40:8

He that doth not forgive burns the bridge over which he himself must needs pass.
—Unknown

_____

_____

_____

_____

_____

_____

_____

_____

_____

_____

_____

_____

_____

_____

_____

_____

_____

_____

_____

_____

_____

SEARCH ME, O GOD, AND KNOW MY HEART; TEST ME AND KNOW MY ANXIOUS THOUGHTS.
SEE IF THERE IS ANY OFFENSIVE WAY IN ME, AND LEAD ME IN THE WAY EVERLASTING.

—Psalm 139:23-24 NIV

Trials teach us what we are; they dig up the soil, and let us see what we are made of.
—Charles Haddon Spurgeon

FOR YOU ARE MY ROCK AND MY FORTRESS; THEREFORE, FOR YOUR NAME'S SAKE, LEAD ME AND GUIDE ME.

—Psalm 31: 3

DO NOT BE OVERCOME WITH EVIL, BUT OVERCOME EVIL WITH GOOD.

—*Romans 12:21*

For God Himself works in our souls, in the deepest depths, taking increasing control as we are progressively willing to be prepared for His wonder.

—Thomas R. Kelly

For what is faith unless it is to believe what you do not see?
—Augustine

_____

_____

_____

_____

_____

_____

_____

_____

_____

GOD,

YOU'RE MY LAST

CHANCE OF THE DAY.

I SPEND THE NIGHT ON

MY KNEES BEFORE YOU.

—*Psalm 88:1*

The Message

_____

_____

_____

_____

_____

_____

At the heart of grace is *giving.* God is the giver of all good things. He delights to lavish blessings upon us. His grace is remarkable evidence of His generosity.

A gracious woman, therefore is a *grace-giver.* She gives willingly—not just materially, but of herself:

Because she receives inexhaustible grace, she can extend grace.

Because she is deeply loved by her Father, she can love others.

Because she is forgiven, she can readily forgive.

Because she hears the Lord speak graciously to her, she can communicate with grace.

Because her strength and peace are from the Lord, she can impart a gentle and quiet spirit to those around her.

Because she is humbled by the privilege of being God's child, she can serve selflessly, delighting in bringing glory to Him alone.

—*Cynthia Heald*

God is the giver of all good things. He delights to lavish blessings upon us. His grace is remarkable evidence of His generosity.

_____

_____

_____

_____

_____

_____

_____

_____

_____

_____

God's heart is the most sensitive and tender of all. No act goes unnoticed, no matter how insignificant or small.
—Richard J. Foster

The greatest day in your life and mine is when we take total responsibility for our attitudes. That's the day we truly grow up.

—John

Maxwell

Even now, two thousand years later, we marvel at the beautiful way God has provided what we need most. Being born again is God's solution to our need for love and life and light.

—Anne Graham Lotz

The spiritual life does not remove us from the world but leads us deeper into it.

—Henri J. M. Nouwen

MY HELP COMES FROM THE LORD, WHO MADE HEAVEN AND EARTH. HE WILL NOT ALLOW YOUR FOOT TO BE MOVED; HE WHO KEEPS YOU WILL NOT SLUMBER.

—Psalm 121:2–3

Every tomorrow has two handles. We can take hold of it with the handle of anxiety or the handle of faith.
—Henry Ward Beecher

Faith goes up the stairs that love has built and looks out the window which hope has opened.
—Charles Haddon Spurgeon

_____
_____
_____
_____
_____
_____
_____
_____
_____
_____
_____
_____
_____
_____
_____
_____
_____
_____
_____
_____
_____
_____

We forget that God is a specialist. He is well able to work our failures into His plans.

—Erwin Lutzer

_____

_____

_____

_____

_____

_____

_____

_____

_____

_____

_____

_____

_____

_____

_____

_____

_____

_____

_____

_____

_____

_____

THEREFORE
THE LORD WAITS
TO BE GRACIOUS TO
YOU; THEREFORE HE
WILL RISE UP TO SHOW
MERCY TO YOU. FOR THE
LORD IS A GOD OF JUS-
TICE; BLESSED ARE ALL
THOSE WHO WAIT
FOR HIM.

—*Isaiah 30:18*
NRSV

Your Own Version

You are writing a Gospel,
A chapter each day,
By deeds that you do,
By words that you say.

Men (and women) read what you write,
Whether faithless or true;
Say, what is the Gospel
According to you?

—*Paul Gilbert*

He who is filled with love is filled with God himself.
—Augustine

_____

_____

_____

_____

_____

_____

_____

_____

_____

_____

_____

_____

_____

I WILL BOTH LIE DOWN IN PEACE, AND SLEEP; FOR YOU ALONE, O LORD, MAKE ME DWELL IN SAFETY.

—Psalm 4:8

Each day the Lord give us brings with it a reason to rejoice.

—Thelma Wells

DO NOT WORRY ABOUT ANYTHING, BUT PRAY AND ASK GOD FOR EVERY THING YOU NEED, ALWAYS GIVING THANKS.

—Philippians 4:6 NCV

_____

_____

_____

_____

_____

_____

_____

_____

_____

_____

_____

_____

_____

_____

_____

_____

_____

_____

_____

_____

_____

_____

_____

_____

_____

_____

_____

Comfort and prosperity have never enriched the world as much as adversity has.

—Billy Graham

_____

_____

_____

_____

_____

_____

_____

_____

_____

_____

_____

_____

_____

_____

_____

_____

_____

_____

_____

_____

AND WHATEVER WE ASK WE RECEIVE FROM HIM, BECAUSE WE KEEP HIS COMMANDMENTS
AND DO THOSE THINGS THAT ARE PLEASING IN HIS SIGHT.

—1 John 3:22

I believe the Bible is the best gift God has ever given to man. All the good from the Savior of the world is communicated to us through this book.

—Abraham Lincoln

CALL UNTO ME, AND I WILL ANSWER THEE, AND SHOW THEE GREAT AND MIGHTY THINGS, WHICH THOU KNOWEST NOT.

—*Jeremiah 33:3 KJV*

As a deer longs for flowing streams, so my soul longs for you, O God.

—*Psalm 42:1* NRSV

I have now concentrated all my prayers into one, and that one prayer is this, that I may die to self, and live wholly to Him.
—Charles Haddon Spurgeon

Prayer is kind of like calling home every day.
—Barbara Johnson

THY WORD
IS A LAMP UNTO
MY FEET, AND A LIGHT
UNTO MY PATH.
—*Psalm 119:105 KJV*

Good Job!

Most of us are good at criticizing ourselves and finding fault with what we have done or failed to do. I'd like to suggest an alternate plan—spend some of your leisure time finding pleasure and satisfaction in what you have done as well as in who and what you are. Sound too liberal? Why? Since when is a good self-esteem liberal?

There are times we need to tell ourselves, "Good job!" when we know that is true. That isn't conceited pride, my friend. It's acknowledging in words the feelings of the heart. The Lord knows we hear more than enough internal putdowns!

Communicating in times of leisure includes self-affirmation, acknowledging, of course, that God ultimately gets the glory. After all, He's the One who makes the whole experience possible.

—Charles R. Swindoll

> *There are times we need to tell ourselves, "Good job!" when we know that is true. That isn't conceited pride, my friend. It's acknowledging in words the feelings of the heart.*

Don't take tomorrow to bed with you.

—Norman Vincent Peale

I WILL
MEDITATE ON YOUR
PRECEPTS, AND
CONTEMPLATE
YOUR WAYS.
—*Psalm 119:15*

You can make more friends in two months by becoming interested in other people than you can in two years by trying to get other people interested in you.

—Dale Carnegie

I do not pray for success. I ask for faithfulness.
—Mother Teresa

_____

_____

_____

_____

_____

_____

_____

_____

_____

_____

_____

_____

_____

_____

_____

_____

_____

_____

_____

_____

_____

_____

_____

_____

_____

_____

BUT THE FRUIT OF THE SPIRIT IS LOVE, JOY, PEACE, PATIENCE, KINDNESS, GOODNESS, FAITH-
FULNESS, GENTLENESS AND SELF-CONTROL.

—*Galatians 5:22-23*

Certain thoughts are prayers. There are moments when, whatever be the attitude of the body, the soul is on its knees.
—Victor Hugo

Do not lose faith in God. The grace He gives will be in direct proportion to the amount of sufferings you must bear. No one else can do this except the Creator who made us and knows how to renew our strength by His grace.

—Francois Fenelon

AS WATER REFLECTS A FACE, SO A MAN'S HEART REFLECTS THE MAN.

—*Proverbs 27:19* NIV

Though
we travel the
world over to find
the beautiful, we must
carry it with us or we
find it not.

—Ralph Waldo
Emerson

*W*hen Jesus takes your hand,
He keeps you tight.
When Jesus keeps you tight,
He leads you through your whole life.
When Jesus leads you through your life,
He brings you safely home.

—*Corrie ten Boom*

TRUST IN HIM AT ALL TIMES, YOU PEOPLE; POUR OUT YOUR HEART BEFORE HIM; GOD IS A REFUGE FOR US.

—*Psalm 62:8*

One can never pay in gratitude; one can pay "in kind"
somewhere else in life.
—Anne Morrow Lindbergh

What lies behind us, and what lies before us are tiny matters compared to what lies within us.
—Ralph Waldo Emerson

IT IS OF THE LORD'S MERCIES THAT WE ARE NOT CONSUMED, BECAUSE HIS COMPASSIONS FAIL NOT. THEY ARE NEW EVERY MORNING: GREAT IS THY FAITHFULNESS.

—*Lamentations 3: 22-23* KJV

I am convinced that many times, in the course of our lives, God challenges us with a golden opportunity, a seemingly impossible hurdle, or a terrible tragedy . . . and how we react —or fail to react — determines the course of our future, almost as if we were involved in some sort of heavenly chess game . . . with our destiny always in the balance.

—Og Mandino

GOD IS OUR REFUGE AND STRENGTH, A VERY PRESENT HELP IN TROUBLE.

—Psalm 46:1

I long to accomplish a great and noble task, but it is my chief duty to accomplish small tasks as if they were great and noble.
—Helen Keller

DO YOUR BEST TO PRESENT YOURSELF TO GOD AS ONE APPROVED, A WORKMAN WHO DOES NOT NEED TO BE ASHAMED AND WHO CORRECTLY HANDLES THE WORD OF TRUTH.

—2 Timothy 2:15 NIV

I THINK HOW MUCH YOU HAVE HELPED ME; I SING FOR JOY IN THE SHADOW OF YOUR PROTECTING WINGS. I FOLLOW CLOSE BEHIND YOU; YOUR STRONG RIGHT HAND HOLDS ME SECURELY.

—Psalm 63:7-8 NLT

Everything that happens is either a blessing which is also a lesson, or a lesson which is also a blessing.

—Polly Berrien Berends

No matter how long you nurse a grudge, it won't get better.
—Unknown

No
EYE HAS SEEN,
NO EAR HAS HEARD,
NO MIND HAS CON-
CEIVED WHAT GOD HAS
PREPARED FOR THOSE
WHO LOVE HIM.
—*1 Corinthians 2:9*
NIV

How long has it been since you let God have you?

I mean really *have* you? How long since you gave Him a portion of undiluted, uninterrupted time listening for His voice? Apparently, Jesus did. He made a deliberate effort to spend time with God.

Spend much time reading about the listening life of Jesus and a distinct pattern emerges. He spent regular time with God, praying and listening. Mark says, "Very early in the morning, while it was still dark, Jesus got up, left the house and went off to a solitary place where he prayed" (Mark 1:35 NIV) . . . .

Let me ask the obvious. If Jesus, the Son of God, the sinless Savior of humankind, thought it worthwhile to clear His calendar to pray, wouldn't we be wise to do the same?

—*Max Lucado*

Spend much time reading about the listening life of Jesus and a distinct pattern emerges. He spent regular time with God, praying and listening.

_____

_____

_____

_____

_____

_____

_____

_____

_____

_____

_____

_____

I expect to pass through life but once. If therefore, there be any kindness I can show, or any good thing I can do to any fellow being, let me do it now, and not defer or neglect it, as I shall not pass this way again.
—William Penn

I don't know the secret of success, but I do know the secret of failure is trying to please everyone.
—Luci Swindoll

WHEN ANXIETY WAS GREAT WITHIN ME, YOUR CONSOLATION BROUGHT JOY TO MY SOUL.

—Psalm 94:19

What you do in your house is worth as much as if you did it up in heaven for our Lord God.

—Martin Luther

THE WOUNDED CRY FOR HELP AND GOD DOES NOT REGARD IT AS FOOLISH.

—*Job 24:12*

If you begin to live life looking for the God that is all around you,
every moment becomes a prayer.
—Frank Bianco

SET YOUR MIND ON THE THINGS ABOVE, NOT ON THE THINGS THAT ARE ON EARTH.

—*Colossians 3:2 NASV*

COME TO ME, ALL YOU WHO LABOR AND ARE HEAVY LADEN, AND I WILL GIVE YOU REST.
TAKE MY YOKE UPON YOU AND LEARN FROM ME, FOR I AM GENTLE AND LOWLY IN HEART,
AND YOU WILL FIND REST FOR YOUR SOULS. FOR MY YOKE IS EASY AND MY BURDEN IS LIGHT.
—MATTHEW 11:28–30

A single grateful thought toward heaven is the most complete prayer.
—Gotthold Lessing

IN THE DAY OF MY TROUBLE I WILL CALL UPON YOU, FOR YOU WILL ANSWER ME.

—*Psalm 86:7*

_Faith
in small things
has repercussions
that ripple all the
way out. In a huge
dark room a little
match can light up
the place._

—Joni Eareckson
Tada

When a loved one is facing a difficult challenge, sometimes the smallest, most insignificant things can give them hope—or push them into despair . . . so it's important to consider carefully—and pray mightily about—the ways to reach out to those in need.

The truth is, sometimes we share hope without saying a word. Sometimes we inspire others to hold on in frightening circumstances simply by continuing to live as though the circumstances *aren't* frightening—as though we know everything's going to be all right.

Because we do! That's the hope God has given us. . . .God's promises give us the confidence and reassurance we need to bring hope to others, whether it's in the words we say, in the actions we take, or in the peaceful beauty of His empowering love we wear on our faces.

—*Barbara Johnson*

God's promises give us the confidence and reassurance we need to bring hope to others, whether it's in the words we say, in the actions we take, or in the peaceful beauty of His empowering love we wear on our faces.

In ordinary life we hardly realize that we receive a great deal more than we give, and that it is only with gratitude that life becomes rich.

—Dietrich Bonhoeffer

The best measure of a spiritual life is not its ecstasies, but its obedience.

—Oswald Chambers

THIS BOOK OF THE LAW SHALL NOT DEPART FROM YOUR MOUTH, BUT YOU SHALL MEDITATE IN IT DAY AND NIGHT.

—Joshua 1:8

Remember, God hears our needs and answers our prayers in the manner that will help us serve His will.
—Max Lucado

_____

_____

_____

_____

_____

_____

_____

_____

_____

_____

_____

_____

_____

_____

_____

_____

_____

_____

A FRIENDLY SMILE MAKES YOU HAPPY, AND GOOD NEWS MAKES YOU FEEL STRONG.

—*Proverbs 15:30* CEV

Love is the only thing that we can carry with us when we go, and it makes the end so easy.
—Louisa May Alcott

SO NOW I AM GIVING YOU A NEW COMMANDMENT: LOVE EACH OTHER. JUST AS I HAVE LOVED YOU, YOU SHOULD LOVE EACH OTHER.

—John 13:34 NLT

_____

_____

_____

_____

_____

_____

_____

_____

_____

_____

_____

_____

_____

_____

_____

_____

_____

_____

_____

_____

_____

_____

NOW FAITH IS THE SUBSTANCE OF THINGS HOPED FOR, THE EVIDENCE OF THINGS NOT SEEN.

—Hebrews 11:1

The best portion of a good man's life is his little, nameless,
unremembered acts of kindness and of love.
—William Wordsworth

God is in control, and therefore in everything I can give thanks —not because of the situation but because of the One who directs and rules over it.

—Kay Arthur

_____

_____

_____

_____

_____

_____

_____

_____

_____

_____

_____

_____

_____

_____

_____

_____

_____

_____

_____

_____

_____

DELIGHT
YOURSELF ALSO
IN THE LORD, AND
HE SHALL GIVE YOU
THE DESIRES OF YOUR
HEART.

—*Psalm 37:4*

Perhaps you are facing

a tough decision. You may not know which of two opportunities to choose . . . Take your difficulty to the God of wisdom and spread your situation before Him. Divest your own will and solemnly desire to know God's will. Then expect to have an answer from the Most High. Make your prayer the one that the boy Samuel prayed: "Speak, Lord, for Your servant hears." . . . Do not ask God to confirm your opinion; ask Him to make your opinion conform to His truth.

Follow the simple Word of God as you find it. Let the Holy Spirit flow on the sacred page, and as you read you will hear the Master say, "This is My Word." He will make it come to your soul with power. You will have no doubt when your heart cries, "Speak Lord, for Your servant hears."

—*Charles Haddon Spurgeon*

Take your difficulty to the God of wisdom and spread your situation before Him. Divest your own will and solemnly desire to know God's will. Then expect to have an answer from the Most High.

The goal of the Christian life is to be restored to God's likeness, to be holy as God is holy, to be like Christ in character.

—Jerram Barrs and Ranald Macaulay

MEDITATE

WITHIN YOUR HEART

ON YOUR BED, AND BE

STILL.

—*Psalm 4:4*

Adversity is always unexpected and unwelcomed. It is an intruder and a thief, and yet in the hands of God, adversity becomes the means through which His supernatural power is demonstrated.

—Charles Stanley

A smile is the lighting system of the face and the heating system of the heart.

—Barbara Johnson

THUS I WILL BLESS YOU WHILE I LIVE; I WILL LIFT UP MY HANDS IN YOUR NAME.

—Psalm 63:4

_____

_____

_____

_____

_____

_____

_____

_____

_____

_____

_____

_____

_____

_____

_____

_____

_____

_____

_____

_____

_____

_____

The universe is but one vast symbol of God.
—Thomas Carlyle

JESUS ANSWERED, "I AM THE WAY AND THE TRUTH AND THE LIFE. NO ONE COMES TO THE FATHER EXCEPT THROUGH ME.

—John 14:6 NIV

THE LORD IS MY LIGHT AND MY SALVATION; WHOM SHALL I FEAR? THE LORD IS THE
STRENGTH OF MY LIFE; OF WHOM SHALL I BE AFRAID?

—Psalm 27:1

Heaven will be inherited by every man who has heaven in his soul.
—Henry Ward Beecher

My heart leaps up when I behold a rainbow in the sky.
—William Wordsworth

A very sincere and thoughtful Christian knows he can no more get along without faith than a fish can survive out of water. But the question is how does one get this faith . . . this ability to trust God actively whom our five senses cannot perceive.

Have you ever asked God for the gift of faith? Or is this so obvious you've overlooked it. Be sure, however, that you really want what you ask for. Praying can be "dangerous business." If you ask for piano lessons, you'll have to do some practicing. If you ask for faith, you'll probably encounter situations immediately that will call for complete trust in God alone.

—*Catherine Marshall*

Have you ever asked God for the gift of faith? Or is this so obvious you've over-looked it. Be sure, however, that you really want what you ask for.

God loves you right where you are but he doesn't want to leave you there.

—Max Lucado

I

LOVE THOSE

WHO LOVE ME

AND THOSE WHO

DILIGENTLY SEEK WILL

FIND ME.

—*Proverbs 8:17*

What else is nature but God?

—Seneca

Patience is the companion of wisdom.
—Augustine

THE HAND OF OUR GOD IS UPON ALL THOSE FOR GOOD WHO SEEK HIM, BUT HIS POWER
AND HIS WRATH ARE AGAINST ALL THOSE WHO FORSAKE HIM.

—Ezra 8:22

How far you go in life depends on you being tender with the young, compassionate with the aged, sympathetic with the striving, and tolerant of the weak and the strong. Because someday in life you will have been all of these.
—George Washington Carver

IN HIM WE HAVE REDEMPTION THROUGH HIS BLOOD, THE FORGIVENESS OF SINS, ACCORDING TO THE RICHES OF HIS GRACE.

—*Ephesians 1:7*

THE HEAVENS DECLARE THE GLORY OF GOD; AND THE FIRMAMENT SHOWS HIS HANDIWORK.

—*Psalm 19:1*

One with God is a majority.

—Billy Graham

We should be careful not to give all our time to just reading the Word, to see how much we can cover, but, after reading a portion, we should carefully, prayerfully turn it over in our minds, and appropriate it in our hearts.

—Wilber M. Smith

_____

_____

_____

_____

_____

_____

_____

_____

_____

_____

_____

_____

_____

_____

_____

_____

_____

_____

Jesus promised that the Spirit

would guide believers in *the way of all truth (John 16:13)*. Thus, the Holy Spirit is charged with the ministry of guiding believers into an experience of truth revealed in Jesus.

How wonderful it is that God has sent His Spirit to guide us in the way of all truth. And how we need to rely on the Spirit each day of our lives. We need His wisdom so we might understand how God's truth relates to every aspect of our lives. And we need the strength He provides to enable us to walk in God's ways.

The promised Holy Spirit has come. He continues to speak within our hearts, showing us the way that we are to walk in Jesus' truth. We need only to reach out, relying on God's Spirit to provide the guidance we need.

—*Larry Richards*

How wonderful it is that God has sent His Spirit to guide us in the way of all truth.

We need to stop looking at work as simply a means of earning a living and start realizing it is one of the elemental ingredients of making a life.

—Luci Swindoll

Life
is what we
make it, always has
been, always will be.

—Grandma Moses

I AM YOUR SERVANT; GIVE ME UNDERSTANDING, THAT I MAY KNOW YOUR TESTIMONIES.

—Psalm 119:125

Do all the good you can. By all the means you can. In all the ways you can. In all the places you can. At all the times you can. To all the poeple you can. As long as ever you can.

—John Wesley

THESE COMMANDMENTS THAT I GIVE YOU TODAY ARE TO BE UPON YOUR HEARTS. IMPRESS THEM ON YOUR CHILDREN. TALK ABOUT THEM WHEN YOU SIT AT HOME AND WHEN YOU WALK ALONG THE ROAD, WHEN YOU LIE DOWN AND WHEN YOU GET UP.

—Deuteronomy 6:6-7 NIV

We are not human beings on a spiritual journey. We are spiritual beings on a human journey.

—Stephen Covey

AND WHATEVER THINGS YOU ASK IN PRAYER, BELIEVING, YOU WILL RECEIVE.

—Matthew 21:22

People see God every day, they just don't recognize him.
—Pearl Bailey

Faith is the conviction that God knows more than we do about this life and He will get us through it.

–Max Lucado

When one door of happiness closes, another opens; but often we look so long at the closed door that we do not see the one which has been opened for us.

—Helen Keller

Acknowledgments

Grateful acknowledgment is made to the following for permission to reprint copyrighted material:

Adventurous Prayer © 2003, excerpted by permission of Thomas Nelson Publishers.

Checklist for Life© 2002 GRQ, Inc., excerpted by permission of Thomas Nelson Publishers.

Donelson Fellowship, The ©2004, *Pocket Papers, http://www.donelson.org/pocket.cfm.*

Cynthia Heald, excerpted by permission of Thomas Nelson Publishers from the book entitled
Becoming a Woman of Faith © 2000.
— *Becoming a Woman of Grace* © 1998, excerpted by permission of Thomas Nelson Publishers.

Barbara Johnson, excerpted by permission of W Publishing Group, a division of Thomas Nelson
Publishers from the book entitled *The Great Adventure* © 2002.
—*Devotions for a Sensational Life* © 2002, excerpted by permission of Thomas Nelson
Publishers.
—*Daily Splashes of Joy* © 2000, excerpted by permission of W Publishing Group, a division of
Thomas Nelson Publishers.
—*Irrespressible Hope,* © 2003, excerpted by permission of W Publishing Group, a division of
Thomas Nelson Publishers © 2003.

Nicole Johnson, excerpted by permission of W Publishing Group, a division of Thomas Nelson
Publishers from the book entitled *Irrepressible Hope* © 2002.

Anne Graham Lotz, excerpted by permission of W Publishing Group, a division of Thomas Nelson
Publishers from the book entitled *Just Give Me Jesus* © 2003 by Anne Graham Lotz.

Max Lucado, excerpted by permission of J. Countryman, a division of Thomas Nelson Publishers
from the book entitled *Grace for the Moment* © 2002.
—*In the Grip of Grace* © 1996 by Max Lucado, excerpted by permission of W Publishing Group,
a division of Thomas Nelson Publishers.
—*A Gentle Thunder* © 1995, by Max Lucado, excerpted by permission of W Publishing Group, a
division of Thomas Nelson Publishers.

Catherine Marshall, excerpted by permission of J. Countryman, a division of Thomas Nelson
Publishers from the book entitled *Moments That Matter* © 2001 by Marshall-LeSourd LLC.

John C. Maxwell, excerpted by permission of J. Countryman, a division of Thomas Nelson Publishers
from the book entitled *Leadership*© 2001 by John C. Maxwell.

Prayer Requests

Prayer Requests

Prayers Answered

Prayers Answered

Scriptures to Read and Remember

Scriptures to Read and Remember